The Gentlemen's Commandments
Songs for Love, Healing, Freedom, and Purpose

30 DAILY DEVOTIONS

By: Jasmine Jones

The Commandments Series

Dedication

To all the *Gentlemen* who asked,

"Where's your book for guys?"

My dedication for the second installment in

The Commandments Series (albeit completely unforeseen)

belongs to you.

To the closest *Gentlemen* in my life, my Dad and my two

brothers–Cyrus and Dominic, I hope this book inspires you

too!

This book is for you!

Table of Contents

Introduction

Why **30** songs? Why a **30**-day guide for love, healing, freedom, and purpose? The answer lies in this, *Gentlemen*, the number **30** symbolizes a commitment to a calling or task.

What do Joseph, King David, John the Baptist, and Jesus all have in common? You guessed it, the number **30**. Each of these men reached a level of physical and mental maturity calling them to their divine purpose at age **30**.

This **30** day-devotional commits you to a level of responsibility. It requires you to dedicate your time to take ownership of your own love life, rectify your own healing, and make the conscious choice to live in freedom with a divine purpose. Imagine gaining the knowledge to live according to your God-given calling. Imagine having the power and wisdom to embrace your life's learned lessons. What better way to make your imagination a reality than through music?

These daily devotions are designed to inspire you to embrace and manage your life's experiences through the artistic medium of music. Think about it. At some point or another, music have roused just about every emotion from inside of you–laughter, sadness, fury, joy, and pain. Music

1

urges you to dance and sing, and it serves as a personal reflection of your everyday life. From this devotional book, you will learn to engage a great familiarity to you, that familiarity is your interest and love for music. You'll then use your knowledge to embrace the love of God in your life and enhance your spiritual journey.

This guide illustrates daily applicative examples to help you achieve and fulfill *The Gentlemen's Commandments*, the second installment in the Commandments Series. Memorize your *Gentlemen's Commandments* and apply them to your daily walk, experiences, and encounters. As you read each of your **30** devotions, reference the following commandments:

Commandment #1: Thou shall *love* God and thyself.
Commandment #2: Thou shall seek spiritual *healing*.
Commandment #3: Thou shall live in *freedom* from temptation.
Commandment #4: Thou shall trust God for divine *purpose*.

Each daily devotion is comprised of three main sections: **Listen**, **Read**, and **Reference**.

For each daily devotion, you are encouraged to seek a reliable, lawful, and permissible music listening application and listen to a radio edited or clean version of the listed song.

2

If you have access to Spotify or Apple Music, you may choose to subscribe to www.jasminejones.co for a website link to *The Gentlemen's Commandments* playlist, which includes a collection of songs in this book. Keep in mind additional subscription rates to the music listening application may apply.

Following the music, you will read the daily devotion for understanding and reference the biblical scripture. You are encouraged to reference the source of all the biblical scriptures for further personal study.

Gentlemen, be prepared for the next **30** days of responsibility as God teaches you to draw closer to Him and walk wisely in your calling.

I am weary, O God;
I am weary and worn out, O God.
I am too stupid to be human,
and I lack common sense.
I have not mastered human wisdom,
nor do I know the Holy One. . .
There are three things that amaze me—
no, four things that I don't understand:
how an eagle glides through the sky,
how a snake slithers on a rock,

how a ship navigates the ocean,

how a man loves a woman.

– Proverbs **30**:1-3, 18-19 (NLT)

Commandment #1

Love

Thou shall *love* God and thyself.

Day 1: The Wait

Listen

Michael Jackson – You Are Not Alone (1995)

Read

A *Gentlemen* friend once enlightened me, "finding a wife is hard work."

"Harder than a woman waiting for a husband?" I questioned. I approached the judge's bench to present my case on behalf of women around the world.

The Holy Bible instructs women to *wait*. The book of Proverbs teaches us that *he who finds a wife finds a good thing* (Proverbs 18:22 NKJV).

The keyword in this biblical scripture is "he." That means as *Single Ladies*, we aren't roaming and searching the earth for a husband. For the men who always thought the playing field should be equal and women should be searching high and low for you, sorry to disappoint you, *fellas*.

Of course, *Single Ladies* have a choice in the matter. We decide if you are indeed *Gentlemen* who we want to date. Until then, we as women are instructed to *wait*. We are waiting for you to seek so that we may be found. While you, *Gentlemen*, have the ability to put a plan into action, we *wait*. While you go out and pursue, we wait. We wait for a man who exhibits God's characteristics. Quite frankly, in the process, we sometimes become battered, tired, and occasionally even bitter. However, that's a devotion for another day. Today, we are the defendants proving our case.

Speaking from personal experience, as a woman who always has a plan and is ready to execute, this waiting process can be challenging. All things considered, if we really look at this *thing* from your perspective, I must admit I'm quite relieved you have the job to find us and not the other way around. Perhaps I'm not helping my case much with the preceding statement.

The Proverbs scripture under discussion continues and declares when you find a wife it is a tangible sign that you, *Gentlemen, obtain favor from the LORD* (Proverbs 18:22 NKJV). I can only imagine the pressure you must bear.

As I compare roles of men and women, it's very clear that we must both be patient in this regard. *Single Ladies* patiently wait for a God-fearing man and *Gentlemen* patiently seek a God-fearing woman.

Let's just say we're equal. This way I don't have to confess that your role in the love arena just may be *ever so slightly* more difficult. Indeed, you must also wait. You must wait for God's perfect timing.

In all your waiting, don't forget God is always accessible and available to help you. God will not leave you alone! He is here for you. If you follow His instructions, you will know when He instructs you to seek, and He'll confirm *when* you find love. There's no secret this wait requires strength. *This wait* requires courage. Since you've agreed to read this book and follow God on this 30-day journey, I'm confident that you'll find your strength to wait on the Lord.

Reference

Be of good courage,

And He shall strengthen your heart,

All you who hope in the Lord.

– Psalm 31:24 (NKJV)

Day 2: I'm Ready

Listen

Alicia Keys feat. Drake – Un-thinkable (I'm Ready) (2009)

Read

Let's have a heart-to-heart, *Gentlemen.* We're talking about love, so matters of the heart should be no problem to discuss here. I have two very important questions to ask you.

1) What is love?

2) Are you ready for love?

I'll give you a moment to ponder on these questions. Do you have your responses? Yes? Great!

Now let's see if you passed my test. What is love? God describes *love* so genuinely and in its purest form in the first book of Corinthians. Love *is patient, kind, not boastful, or rude* (1 Corinthians 13:4-5 NLT). Jesus instructed us, *you shall love the Lord your God with all your heart, with all your soul, with all your mind, and with all your strength. . . you shall love your neighbor as yourself. There is no other commandment greater than these* (Mark 12:30-31 NKJV). Jesus further explained that we should even love our enemies (Matthew 5:44).

Gentlemen, was this your definition of love? Were you close? Now, I'm going to get a little personal. Do you exhibit the characteristics of *love*, not just to your family and friends, but to all? Is your love sincere? Does your love endure all?

I once accompanied a guy on a first date. We were walking from a restaurant in a shopping district to his car when he spotted three unaccompanied children wandering after dark. He seemed very concerned for these lonely children. I'm not going to lie; my first thought: *why is this man so concerned? I hope he's not concerned for these children for the wrong reasons.*

Forgive me. Remember that battered and tired woman I spoke of in yesterday's devotion? It wasn't too long ago that I was that woman. During this time, my thoughts would instantly become pessimistic before they found the silver lining.

With that being said, once I forced myself out of my own thoughts and engaged in my current situation, I realized this guy genuinely cared for people who may not be able to care for themselves. As we continued to walk through the shopping district, we noticed the children enter a hotel lobby and we assumed that their family was residing in a hotel room for the weekend.

Gentlemen, are you like this man? Do you love God and His people? How do you exhibit this love? Keep in mind if you demonstrate love for God's people, you'll attract love in all arenas of your life. This includes the possibility of *romantic* love (just something to consider).

Now to my second question. Are you ready for love? If you're a man who truly desires to be a husband one day, you may fear that you'll be searching this earth forever for a wife. You don't want to share Drake's sentiment of turning 30 years old, or a few years after 30 wondering if you'll be single forever. I have to assume that since you're reading this book, you are indeed ready for love.

What are you doing to prove this desire? Do you know what it takes to love a wife? I'll tell you what. I'll give you a day to think about the boat you find yourself in and tomorrow I'll share insight on how you can exhibit that God-defined love. Deal?

Reference

Love is patient and kind. Love is not jealous or boastful or proud or rude. It does not demand its own way. It is not irritable, and it keeps no record of being wronged. It does not rejoice about injustice but rejoices whenever the truth wins out. Love never gives up, never loses faith, is always hopeful, and endures through every circumstance.

– 1 Corinthians 13:4-7 (NLT)

Day 3: Chivalry is Dead

Listen

Panic! At the Disco – Death of a Bachelor (2016)

Read

Salt water and rubbish are all around you. The nearest land is over four-hundred miles south of you and you find yourself amidst two-thousand other passengers and crew in the North Atlantic Ocean. Where are we, *Gentlemen?*

I'll give you another hint. It's the early morning hours of April 15, 1912 and we have the unfortunate circumstances of being shipwrecked. The worst part of it all, we are only four days into our voyage, traveling the unchartered seas aboard the *Titanic.*

Well technically, now we are floating just like Leonardo DiCaprio and Rose, professionally known as Kate Winslet, atop a mutilated wooden door that broke apart during the ship's collision with an iceberg. For those of us who are familiar with the tragedy of the Titanic, we know how this story ends. That's right, with a bachelor's untimely death.

Many people have argued that Rose could have shared that broken door with DiCaprio. I actually agree.

12

However, today we will not dispute this debate. We will only assume that there was absolutely no room on the door for this bachelor, or that there was no other wreckage he could have laid upon to save his own life.

Now that our scene is set, let's revisit our question from yesterday. Let's talk about your boat, *Gentlemen*. Are you, sir, ready for love? In our day and age, too many times we hear the saying *chivalry is dead.*

As God-fearing women, we are waiting for a husband who loves God first and loves us as God does. God loves both men and women so much He was willing to send His only begotten son, Jesus, to die for our sins (John 3:16). This is the greatest form of chivalry.

Like God, you should not leave your woman in times of trouble (Deuteronomy 31:8). If necessary, in times of danger, you should be willing to lay down your life for her. This is true chivalry; any man can open doors, pull out a chair, or pay for a date. These qualities are appreciated, but a man who demonstrates true chivalry is a man of valor. A man of valor is willing to protect and defend the woman he loves at all costs.

Maybe you should stop to think about how chivalry died. Perhaps chivalry died because men were just too chivalrous. As in the case of DiCaprio's character, chivalry died both literally and figuratively with his death.

Perhaps not as extreme as physical death. Let's consider what it means to relinquish your *most-prized* bachelor title. Are you willing to let go of your casual dating? Are you willing to surrender your love for the chase? Are you ready to forgo flirting with other women for the purpose of collecting their number and calling them later? Again, I ask, are you ready for love, *Gentlemen?*

Reference

For God so loved the world that He gave His only begotten Son, that whoever believes in Him should not perish but have everlasting life.

– John 3:16 (NKJV)

Day 4: Sold Out

Listen

Drake – Fake Love [Clean] (2016)

Read

Judas Iscariot showed fake love toward Jesus and sold him out for thirty pieces of silver. Never doubt the value of a dollar or silver in this case. Judas was Jesus' follower, His disciple, and His friend. If people were willing to betray Jesus, the Son of God; who died on the cross for our sins, trust me, *Gentlemen,* you will experience fake love too.

Pray for God's wisdom to guide you. Just because your fake cousin, Mookie, has known you since you were three-years-old and have always been there, it doesn't mean he needs to continue to have an active role in your life. If Mookie is taking advantage of you, it may be time to let him exit stage left in your life.

Love doesn't just apply to finding *romantic love,* but finding out how to best love yourself. It's true God called us to love one another, but you can love some people from afar. If you find yourself lacking genuine brotherhood, find yourself seeking love in a brother that sticks closer than a friend (Proverbs 18:24). Who is this friend? This friend is Jesus.

If you desire Christ-like friends, be the kind of friend you want to be. Show yourself as friendly and true exhibiting the love of Jesus (Proverbs 18:24).

Remember, God loved you so much that He sent His son Jesus to die on the cross for your sins (John 3:16)? Now that *Gentlemen* is love in its most genuine form.

Jesus was whipped and beaten. He bled and He died just for you. Do you know if you were the only person on this earth, Jesus would have still died just for you? You can honor Him through being fully sold out for Him. In other words, dedicating your life to God to the point where no one can bribe you to live otherwise.

If you find yourself struggling with identifying who is genuinely loving you, or with disowning a person who is not loving you by God's definition–do you yourself a favor, *Gentlemen,* and let that person go. Ask God for wisdom on how to decipher between those who are fake and real. Ask God for strength to release yourself from *friendships* that are toxic to you.

Remember, *love is patient, kind, not boastful, or rude* (1 Corinthians 13:4-5 NLT). Pray for this true love to surround you daily.

Reference

"A new commandment I give to you, that you love one another; as I have loved you, that you also love one another. By this all will know that you are My disciples, if you have love for one another."

– John 13:34-35 (NKJV)

74747525755547

Day 5: Sweet Heart

Listen

Brandy feat. Chris Brown – Put It Down (2012)

Read

If you play your cards right, you might just find love. If you have a sweet heart, *Sweetheart,* you may just fall in love.

A *sweet heart* is a heart like David's. David was a king who had many eye-opening and shocking faults. Yet, God declared that David was a man after His own heart (Acts 13:22).

David's father had seven sons, the youngest being David, who merely tended to sheep (1 Samuel 16:10-11). David was considered among the least of his brothers in terms of physical stature, but God chose and anointed David as king (1 Samuel 16:7). A king is often regarded as physically strong and powerful, so why did God choose David? Here's the answer: God looks at the heart and God had a clear scope into David's heart.

The husband God created you to be is a gentleman after God's own heart. That means you desire to live a life daily that is pleasing in the Lord's sight. You are so in tuned with God that you think like God. You have the aptitude and the ability to choose a virtuous woman, who is also following

18

God. You will see more than just her outer appearance. More importantly, you'll see her inner beauty–her heart.

This means that you, *Gentlemen*, need to learn how to detect good fruit, and you also need to bear good fruit. What do I mean? What fruit? I'll give you a hint. It's not apples, oranges, or pears.

This fruit is a definite sign of one's true intentions. God calls men and women to yield all nine attributes of the fruit of the Spirit: *love, joy, peace, patience, kindness, goodness, faithfulness, gentleness, and self-control. There is no law against these things* (Galatians 5:22-23 NLT).

If you're not yielding these good fruits, you're a direct reflection of your seed. Perhaps you didn't water or feed your seed with the proper nutrients to produce good fruit. Jesus enlightened us when He explained that a good tree couldn't produce bad fruit (Matthew 7:18). If you are a good tree, your fruit will likewise be good.

You have to be aware of the fruit you attract as well. Don't just pay attention to your yielding fruit, but take the time to identify the fruit of the woman you are interested in. Confirm that her fruit is as sweet as she claims it to be.

Reference

" . . . For the Lord does not see as man sees; for man looks at the outward appearance, but the Lord looks at the heart."

– 1 Samuel 16:7 (NKJV)

Day 6: Yo-az (Where's my Ruth?)

Listen

Kendrick Lamar – DNA. [Clean] (2017)

Read

What's in your DNA? As men of God, you have royalty inside your DNA. Scientifically speaking, DNA carries your genetic makeup, determines your growth, and dictates how your body functions, but do you also have loyalty in your DNA?

As women, sometimes we are loyal to a fault. This loyalty comes at the cost of being faithful to men who don't deserve our faithfulness. These men are the ones who find themselves in *committed* relationships and marriages, but still seek other women. Leading many of us women to believe that all men cheat. Leaving us women questioning why he pursuits us when he knows he has a woman.

However, I give you the benefit of the doubt, *Gentlemen.* You desire to love like God loves, so I know that even if you were once this man, you will make the conscious decision not to take advantage of a faithful woman who resembles Ruth.

If you desire a wife, but you're not sure what qualities

21

she should possess, believe me, *Gentlemen* you want to get you a Ruth. She was only one of two women to have her name grace a book of the Holy Bible. Ruth's husband passed away, yet she chose to return to Bethlehem with her mother-in-law, Naomi, instead of returning to her home (Ruth 1:5, Ruth 1:16-17). Ruth's faithfulness gave her favor with Boaz, a wealthy man, who showed kindness toward a meager Ruth (Ruth 2:1, Ruth 2:10-16).

At least two seasons had passed, still Ruth did not lose faith God would bless her with another husband (Ruth 2:23). As her mother-in-law instructed, Ruth exhibited faith and laid at Boaz's feet all night showing loyalty to him (Ruth 3:4, Ruth 3:14). Boaz recognized her faithfulness. He married Ruth and from their union, they were blessed with a son (Ruth 4:13). Perhaps you've heard *Single Ladies* ask *God where's my Boaz?* Well you, *Gentlemen*, certainly have the potential to be that woman's Boaz.

Boaz is no different than you and God is perfectly capable of blessing you with your Ruth. Except first, you must recognize Boaz was genuinely kind to Ruth before she laid at his feet. First and foremost, exhibit the kindness and loyalty inside your DNA. Allow it to radiate from the inside out. Respect that woman's faithfulness and her covenant with God.

Then, when you meet and commit to your Ruth, be faithful and diligent in respecting the covenant you have with her. This means no entertaining other women romantically as your side chicks, friends, or even acquaintances. If you don't want to give up those situations, then don't waste a faithful woman's time. She is waiting for her Boaz, not Yo-az.

Reference

"I go the way of all the earth; be strong, therefore, and prove yourself a man. And keep the charge of the Lord your God: to walk in His ways, to keep His statutes, His commandments, His judgments, and His testimonies. . . that you may prosper in all that you do and wherever you turn; that the Lord may fulfill His word which He spoke concerning me, saying, 'If your sons take heed to their way, to walk before Me in truth with all their heart and with all their soul,' He said, 'you shall not lack a man on the throne. . .'"
– 1 Kings 2:2-4 (NKJV)

Day 7: Dear King

Listen
Miguel – Coffee [Clean] (2015)

Read
That small, brown, roasted nugget transforms from a grounded substance to liquid magic in your cup. Even if you're not a fan of coffee, you can relate to having a pick me up. Some mornings are quite simply put–rough! Maybe you tossed and turned all night and didn't sleep well. Perhaps you purposely stayed up all night partying on a work night, binge watching an original Netflix series, or indulging in a championship sports game. Quite possibly, you're just not a morning person. Whatsoever you did the night before, you know being a night owl can you leave you drowsy and sluggish.

In this case, what's *your coffee* in the morning? If it's not Folgers or Starbucks, you still need what that *cup of Joe* represents.

I encourage you to find your jolt of energy in God. You don't need a *latte*. Ok, *I know*, corny joke. What I mean is–wake up each morning with a fresh breath thanking God for another day and another chance at life. When you finally stop pushing the snooze button and drag yourself out of bed, find ways to seek God. Involve God in your decisions. Ask for His guidance to make wise decisions in your day.

Consider the wisest of kings. Solomon was a wise king, but we must recall the source of Solomon's wisdom. Solomon received his appointment as a wise judge from the Lord (1 Kings 3:11). Solomon asked God for His wisdom to govern people (1 Kings 3:9). One of Solomon's wisest decrees involved two women who each had a son, but one son died in the night because his mother laid on him (1 Kings 3:19). Both women claimed to be the biological mother of the remaining living son (1 Kings 20-22).

King Solomon resolved their dispute and deciphered the biological mother of the child with ease and sensibility. He declared that the child would be divided in half with a sword so the two women could share him (1 King 3:25). While one woman was perfectly satisfied with the ruling, the other begged the king to give the child to the other woman in an effort to save the child's life (1 Kings 3:26). King Solomon was quickly able to identify the biological mother of the child as the woman who loved the child and pleaded for his life (1 King 3:27).

Gentlemen, I encourage you to be a king. Be a man of wisdom, judging only as God appoints you to judge. When he instructs you to judge, rule in the Holy Spirit with wisdom and love. Understand that God will judge you with the same standard in which you judge (Matthew 7:1-2).

When you wake up groggy in the morning, don't forget to take a moment for self-reflection. When you are called to make wise decisions, confirm that you take ownership of your faults. Sometimes we recognize a criticality in someone else because we identify a familiarity within ourselves.

Jesus asked, "Why worry about a speck in your friend's eye when you have a log in your own?" (Matthew 7:3 NLT). *Gentlemen,* remember to ask yourself this question as well.

Reference

Do not judge others, and you will not be judged. For you will be treated as you treat others. The standard you use in judging is the standard by which you will be judged.
– Matthew 7:1-2 (NLT)

Commandment #2

Healing

Thou shall seek spiritual *healing*.

Day 8: Money, Power, and Respect

Listen

Kanye West feat. Jamie Foxx – Gold Digger (2005)

Read

Delilah was after money, gold, riches, power, respect, and anything else betraying Samson could offer her. Delilah was a woman who deceived Samson into surrendering His God-given power. Day after day, Delilah begged Samson to tell her the secret of his strength and each day Samson would lie to Delilah (Judges 16:6-14). Delilah would unknowingly share false secrets of his power with the Philistines, who would attempt to capture Samson, but inevitably failed (Judges 16: 6-14).

Like many men who claim 'we' women nag them to death, Samson grew tired of Delilah's daily nagging and revealed the true secret of his strength (Judges 16:16-17). Samson's secret was in his hair (Judges 16:17). In his sleep, Delilah had someone shave Samson's hair and the strength of the Lord left him (Judges 16:19). When the Philistines returned, they were able to capture Samson and take out his eyes (Judges 16:21). For her betrayal, the Philistines rewarded Delilah with silver (Judges 16:18).

Fear of gold or *silver* diggers–is one risk that may make it challenging for you, *Gentlemen*, to find a wife. It's true some women don't have the best intentions. I've never been a woman with much of a poker face to play this card game, but some women have the potential of an Oscar winning actress. These women possess the talent to pull the wool right over your eyes, or in Samson's case take your eyes right out of your sockets! Some men have a natural intuitive sense to weed out these women. This intuitive sense is called discernment. Do you have it? Yes? Well that's great.

If not, ask God to grant you discernment to understand a woman's true intentions. God knows all and sees all. He's omniscient and He can help you decipher between a deceiving *Delilah* and a faithful *Ruth*. Seeking God in every dating situation can save you a lot of heartbreak and headache and it can definitely save your pockets!

Reference

Therefore give to Your servant an understanding heart to judge Your people, that I may discern between good and evil…

– 1 Kings 3:9 (NKJV)

Day 9: Wifey For Lifey

Listen

Next – Wifey (2000)

Read

Wifey is a woman who is *wife-like*. She is a woman with whom you are not completely committed to and have not *put a ring on it*. She may have the qualities of a woman you would like to *wife*, but you haven't taken the plunge to actually make it legal on paper or in the eyes of God.

Gentlemen, have you ever feared the idea of marriage? Think about it. If the marriage is God-ordained, the marriage is the end all be all. That means you're committing your life to one person forever, or at least until death do you part. That can be a scary thought.

There are over 7 billion people in this world. When two people decide to marry, they are standing before God and law to bind themselves to each other for the rest of their lives. Getting out of this marriage is no easy task. For one, it can cost a lot of bucks to divorce someone. Not to mention if you have children, then it makes it even more difficult to part.

Maybe your fear of marriage stems from your divorced parents or never having a virtuous example of a

30

God-ordained marriage. Whatsoever your reasoning, I would like to encourage you. *God has not given us a spirit of fear, but of power and of love and of a sound mind* (2 Timothy 1:7).

Think of love like precious rubies. If you take rocks to a pawnshop and try to exchange it for rubies, the shop owner will likely laugh in your face. In the same token, if you take fear to the bank and try to exchange it for love, it just won't work! Love and fear are two separate currencies with no existing exchange rate. If you fear a marriage will hurt you because you were hurt in the past, you close off your heart to love.

Don't exchange a wife with *wifey for lifey* in fear of having nothing at all. Think about it. Why would you give your all to a *wifey*, when you can have favor with the Lord that comes with a wife? *Would you present what is holy to dogs, or offer pearls to a swine* (Matthew 7:6)? Then, why throw away something so precious as a wife for an easy way out.

Take a moment to think about your last relationship with a woman. Why didn't she become your wife? Did you realize that she was a *wifey* and you were willing to let her go to wait for a wife? Just as you exchanged that ex for an opportunity at something better, be willing to exchange a *wifey* in your life for a virtuous woman who's a better fit for you.

Reference

Who can find a virtuous wife?

For her worth is far above rubies.

The heart of her husband safely trusts her;

So he will have no lack of gain.

She does him good and not evil

All the days of her life.

— Proverbs 31:10-12 (NKJV)

Day 10: In Her Shoes

Listen

Daley – Blame The World (2014)

Read

It's better to have loved and lost than to have never loved at all.
Perhaps true, but reflect on the role you played in this love
lost. Who do you blame for this love lost?

Be honest, did you blow it? Did you ruin it? Can you
blame her for not wanting to be with you? If you betrayed her
trust like you betrayed hers, would you really be all ears?
Probably not and you would understand if you really attempt
to take the time to walk in her heels. That's right, I said heels.

She tried everything in her power to fit her *brand-new
shoes*. Those brand-new shoes are symbolic for you in her life.
No matter how hard she tugged and pulled on the laces it was
evident that you weren't willing to put up the same effort to
fit in her life. Consequently, she gave up the fight. She finally
moved on and left you to blame the world.

If you were a man, who wronged this woman, I
would encourage you to apologize to this woman and seek
forgiveness. This is not just any apology. This is a confession

and plea for forgiveness. We will expand on this topic further another day.

For the time being, *Gentlemen*, take responsibility for your actions with this newfound perspective. Understanding that one day you will stand before God and be asked to account for these actions.

Reference

So why do you condemn another believer? Why do you look down on another believer? Remember, we will all stand before the judgment seat of God. . . Yes, each of us will give a personal account to God. So let's stop condemning each other. Decide instead to live in such a way that you will not cause another believer to stumble and fall.

– Romans 14:10, 12-13 (NLT)

Day 11: If

Listen

Bryson Tiller – Sorry Not Sorry [Clean] (2015)

Read

The *if* apology is also known as the non-apology. It's most commonly used in politics as the *sorry, not sorry*. For example, "I'm sorry *if* you were offended." When clearly that person was offended. Otherwise, they wouldn't be bringing it up. Hence, there's no *ifs* about it.

Gentlemen, do you use the *if* apology? Perhaps someone has used the *if* apology with you. As sons of Christ, you are expected to love your enemies and forgive those who persecute you. Jesus was mocked and brutally scorned. Still, before Jesus died on the cross, He pleaded with God, "Father, forgive them, for they don't know what they are doing" (Luke 23:34 NLT). Jesus spoke these words as He witnessed soldiers throw dice, gambling for His clothes (Matthew 27:35).

Tell me, could you have Jesus' heart of forgiveness? Perhaps you at least received the *if* apology. Jesus received no apology and Jesus still forgave these people. Learn to forgive even without an expression of regret from another person.

Ask God for a heart to forgive the people who wrong you.

In the book of Matthew, Peter asked Jesus, "how many times should I forgive?" (Matthew 18:21 NKJV).

Jesus responded, "Up to seventy times seven!" (Matthew 18:22 NKJV).

Do you justify the *if* apology in your own confessions? If your typical method of reparation is the *sorry not sorry*, I encourage you to change your approach. I encourage you to not only sound sincere when you apologize but be sincere.

On the other hand, as iron sharpens iron, we can go to our friends or family if we have a problem with their apology, or lack of apology. It is perfectly acceptable to go to the person in private and seek recompense.

Reference

If another believer sins against you, go privately and point out the offense. If the other person listens and confesses it, you have won that person back.

– Matthew 18:15 (NLT)

Day 12: Healing Confessions

Listen

Usher – Confessions Part II (2004)

Read

Confessing your wrongs is never easy. When we confess our indiscretions, we should confess not just to the one we wronged (James 5:16), but also to God (1 John 1:9). You may admit it is already hard enough to confess to just one person. Why should we confess to one another and God?

Understand this, our personal freedom lies in the act of confessing. Have you ever been practically placed under oath on the Bible to keep a secret, but you shared the secret anyway? Maybe you justified telling the secret because you were confident the person you told wouldn't share it with anyone else, or maybe the person didn't know the individuals involved in the secret.

What if confessing your sins resembled the desire you had to share that secret? When you confess to God, you are no longer bound to the sins you committed. Jesus Christ already served as atonement when He died on the cross to save all of us from our sins. Confession is His gift to us. Embrace this beautiful gift of healing.

Can you recall a time a woman hurt you once, or even multiple times, and you shut down to the ideal of love? If she fooled you once, it was shame on her. If she fooled you twice or more, shame on you, right? Did you ever forgive her? There's healing in forgiving others no matter how many times they've wronged you.

Remember, Jesus instructed us to forgive seventy times seven, but this doesn't mean literally count 490 wrongs and don't forgive them upon wrong number 491 (Matthew 18:21). This means forgive without limitation.

Jesus further shares the story of a wicked servant, who owed his master a debt (Matthew 18:23). The servant pleaded with his master and the master agreed to forgive his loan (Matthew 18:27).

The same servant went to his fellow servant and demanded repayment on a loan (Matthew 18:28). The fellow servant could not repay his debt, so the wicked servant sent him to jail (Matthew 18:30). When the master discovered the wicked servant's deeds, he sent the wicked servant to a tortuous fate until his debt was paid in full (Matthew 18:31-34).

Let's face it, no one on this earth is perfect. One of

the hardest things I've found is not asking God for forgiveness, but asking myself for forgiveness. *Gentlemen,* when was the last time you took a deep-hard look at the man in the mirror to ask and reflect on the meaning of sincerely forgiving yourself.

Forgiving yourself is no easy task, especially when that process requires seeking forgiveness from another person. It's easy to say the guilt of not being honest with a loved one will not weigh on you. However, we know all too well that in the act of requesting forgiveness, either from yourself or from someone else, you find your peace; your comfort, your justice, not to mention and probably most importantly, your healing.

Reference

If we confess our sins, He is faithful and just to forgive us our sins and to cleanse us from all unrighteousness.
·– 1 John 1:9 (NKJV)

Day 13: Open-heart Surgery

Listen

Trey Songz – Heart Attack [Clean] (2012)

Read

Too many times it has become evident to you that the woman you dated is not your God-ordained wife. These women possess wifely qualities you desire, but still her piece doesn't quite fit in your puzzle.

God knows you're alone like Adam, but He doesn't intend for you to be lonely. This is the reason God made Eve–a woman from a man's very own rib.

As men, you may not be so willing to admit it, but sometimes you need healing from past dating experiences. Sometimes that spiritual healing is just what you need to move to the next step in your life and meet your God-ordained woman.

If you believe this describes you, seek God in the areas where you need His healing. Understand everything leading up to your life until now is for God's purpose and glory. God will finish the good work He began in you.

He will not forsake the work of His hands. You are the work of His hands! God's word will not return to him void.

"So shall My word be that goes forth from My mouth;
It shall not return to Me void,
But it shall accomplish what I please,
And it shall prosper *in the thing* for which I sent it" (Isaiah 55:11 NKJV).

At times in life, you may not fully comprehend why you are experiencing certain battles or separations from things you once loved. You may feel conflicted because you're battling between flesh and spirit–a battle between selfish flesh and selfless spirit. Take comfort in that what the enemy meant for evil, God turns around for your good (Genesis 50:20).

Understand when you're faithful to God, He will be faithful to you. If you're holding onto a woman that you know isn't the God-ordained woman for you, be obedient enough to let her go. If you're not sure if she's the woman for you, ask God to reveal it to you. Listen to God and when He reveals the answer, be diligent. He will reward you for your faithfulness.

Make it a priority to guard your heart, *Gentlemen* (Proverbs 4:23). I know sometimes you may feel invincible like Superman, but even you can fall victim to the kryptonite of heartbreak.

God created women from the rib of a man; ribs encase and protect vital organs like the heart. Your future wife is a woman from your very own rib. Like the ribs, she is intended to protect and nurture your heart. When you open up your heart to other women who don't appreciate this responsibility, it can cause your heart to be led astray, down a path that God did not intend. In turn, your heart's reflection will be the painful issues that spring out of your heart (Proverbs 4:23).

If your heart has been jeopardized, engage in some self-reflection and ask God to change your heart. Pray for healing and trust God for your healing. He will be faithful performing a successful *open-heart surgery* and bless you with a new heart.

Reference

I will give you a new heart and put a new spirit within you; I will take the heart of stone out of your flesh and give you a heart of flesh. I will put My Spirit within you and cause you to walk in My statutes, and you will keep My judgments and do *them*.

– Ezekiel 36:26-27 (NKJV)

Day 14: Firestarter

Listen

Usher – Burn (2004)

Read

Can you imagine how God feels when one minute you're metaphorically on fire for Him and the next you're lukewarm or freezing cold? Metaphorically, you emulate fire, all four stages of fire.

First, you're *Ignited*. You hear from God. He grants you a vision and purpose. He ignites you. Secondly, you fuel the heat source; you have a yearning desire to learn more and more. You experience *Growth*. He nurtures you. Next, you're *Fully Developed*. In fact, you're blazing! You find yourself walking in His glory. You reach your highest temperature at this stage. You're a vessel for God.

Then, suddenly you burn out. You become distracted or overwhelmed. Instead of seeking God as your heat source to ignite you again, you *Decay*. All your hard work and invested time is extinguished. Your *flame* is extinguished completely. The first three steps are destroyed in just one stage. You find yourself stagnate. You're not stimulated and you're not progressing either. This is one of the worst feelings

44

in the world–having the desire to grow, but you're stunted.

Ask yourself how are you going to avoid *Decay*, the fourth stage of fire? Ask God to keep you ignited, growing, and fully developed.

If you've ever experienced a breakup from a relationship discerning that without a doubt the relationship was over, you know too well how it felt to let that situation burn. You realized that situation burnt you completely out and you had to tend to the after effects of that fire. You sorted through your thoughts to rebuild yourself and sought healing from the flames that God did not allow to completely consume you.

I challenge you to not be lukewarm (Revelation 3:16). Get that fire started again, but refocus your fire and allow it to burn for God. Take that energy and reignite yourself. Focusing on God as you wait for the woman who will be your help in keeping that fire for God ablaze.

Reference

When you go through deep waters,

    I will be with you.

When you go through rivers of difficulty,

    you will not drown.

When you walk through the fire of oppression,

you will not be burned up;

the flames will not consume you.

– Isaiah 43:2 (NLT)

Commandment #3

Freedom

Thou shall live in *freedom* from temptation.

Day 15: Perfectly Imperfect

Listen

J. Cole feat. Missy Elliott – Nobody's Perfect [Clean] (2011)

Read

I like to think of my transition from girl to woman as a timeless throwback song. I began my journey as an *Around the Way Girl,* as described by LL Cool J, and then blossomed into *I'm Every Woman,* as proclaimed by Whitney Houston.

This evolution didn't happen overnight. It required growth through time and patience. God transformed and developed me. However, I'm not a finished product. I'm not perfect, but He has perfected all things concerning me.

From the time I was a little girl with a family dynamic and upbringing that wasn't so perfect, God kept me. Growing up, I was the eldest child serving as the liaison between two full-grown adults, I called mom and dad.

My parents' divorce wasn't one of those amicable divorces. It was a war and I was Switzerland; a country desiring peace, but stuck in the middle of two countries committed to battling until the bitter end. My divorced parents were the reason I feared marriage. I had a stadium floor seat view to a marriage turned ugly like a *dirty* basketball game.

I believe this first-hand view of *love* turned sour led to my engagement in destructive dating experiences that left me broken-hearted. Still, God perfected every situation in my life.

Obviously, I didn't have perfect parents, like I'm sure many of you, but I still learned to honor them. Jesus told us that honoring our parents was God's highest commandment with promise so that our lives may be long (Ephesians 6:2). This command was imperative to you as boys, and still stands for you as *Gentlemen*.

Gentlemen, I know, like me, you're also timeless. You're a classic *throwback* and like a dj, you throw your own spin on the turn table. You walk into a room with a GQ charisma that demands the attention of the room.

You're not perfect, but trust God will make perfect everything that concerns you too. Sometimes when the stresses and battles of living this imperfect life gets tough, you desire an escape from it all. You may desire a way to unwind and let go of the cares of this world. You may find yourself indulging in destructive substances or activities for a form of escape. I encourage you to cast your cares upon God because He cares for you (Psalm 55:22).

If you seek a high in man-made creations, I persuade you to find your high in the ultimate creator, God. He will always offer you the greatest high of all. He will never forsake you. God knows you're not perfect, but you're perfect for Him and He wants to employ you for His perfect glory. All you have to do is let go and let God use you.

Reference

The Lord will perfect that which concerns me;

Your mercy, O Lord, endures forever;

Do not forsake the works of Your hands.

– Psalm 138:8 (NKJV)

Day 16: Live or Die?

Listen

The Weeknd feat. Drake – Live For [Clean] (2013)

Read

What are you living for? Are you living for your friends? Are you living for your girlfriend or your family? Are you living for the weekend? No pun intended.

God desires that you love life and enjoy it, but be careful who and what you live for. Your actions should honor God and make Him proud to call you His son. Make sure that the things you are living for give God the glory. Above all, confirm that you are living for God first and foremost.

We understand Jesus lived on this earth to provide us with an example of how to live this life. He's a living example of how to live your life as single *Gentlemen*. You understand Jesus lived and died for you.

As *Gentlemen*, you should repay him. You may ask, *repay him? Are you crazy? How could I possibly repay Jesus for all He has done?* Well, I'm so glad you asked! I promise this repayment doesn't end in the untimely death of a bachelor this time.

51

You repay Jesus by living in His image daily. Living in freedom from your past sins. A sin is anything that is displeasing to God. When you dedicate yourself to living for God, you will pray, read your bible, and spend time with God on a daily basis. When you perform these tasks, you'll draw closer to God and He'll draw closer to you (James 4:8). You'll gain a keen sense of what He finds sin and you'll gain a heart that desires to do the things that pleases God.

This doesn't mean you won't slip up or be tempted. Even Jesus was tempted. The devil tempted Jesus, but He did not waiver. After 40 days of fasting, the enemy perceived Jesus' hunger, and thus tempted Jesus to turn rocks into bread (Matthew 4:2-3). The enemy attempted to coerce Jesus to jump off a cliff in an effort to tempt God (Matthew 4:5-6); hoping Jesus would commit suicide, thus defeating our Savior.

The enemy also offered Jesus control of the entire world; all He had to do was worship the enemy (Matthew 4:8-9). Do you see? Jesus can empathize with you. Jesus Christ overcame all these temptations and more. Hence, *Gentlemen,* you are overcomers as well. You have the strength and the ability to overcome all temptations and live just as Jesus did! This means having your flesh's desires die daily so that your spirit may live.

Reference

For if you live according to the flesh you will die; but if by the Spirit you put to death the deeds of the body, you will live.

– Romans 8:13 (NKJV)

Day 17: Game Plan

Listen

The Weeknd – Wicked Games [Clean] (2011)

Read

Admit it, American football is a great game! Some traditional footballers wouldn't agree, but many Americans can agree there is nothing like witnessing 2 teams and 11 players from each team going head-to-head for a chance at that most coveted Super Bowl Championship ring at the end of the season.

Unfortunately, I've yet to witness my team play in a Super Bowl. In fact, no one has. Maybe one day my dear Detroit Lions will find themselves in the promise land. *I digress.*

Today's topic of discussion is games. I don't care how old or young you are, we can all take pleasure in games– whether you're playing yourself, or just a spectator. You may even enjoy playing a sport, a board game, or a child's go-to *hide-and-seek,* but my question is, why, oh why do we play games with hearts? You read that right I said *we.* Unlike NFL games, this is a game both men and women play. Sometimes we play well. Sometimes we lose the game, but that doesn't prevent us from taking our shot at a second chance of playing for someone's heart.

We play the game of *when should I call or text after our first date, or when should I answer or respond to aforementioned call or text.* Honestly, I don't think I have the time or energy to get deep into the rules of engagement, but I will say at some point, *Gentlemen,* you may have to be the bigger person and forfeit on these games.

You may have already learned you don't desire the same things in life. Perhaps she expressed she has no interest in marriage and you do, or she feels God has called her to have children, but you do not feel the same. You may hope and wish that she changes her mind, but ultimately, these decisions are perfectly acceptable choices for both parties. It's up to you to stand steadfast in your desires and also understand what you're not willing to compromise on.

Be honest. Be straightforward and forthcoming. If you realize you no longer have an interest in a woman you're dating, it's time to throw a flag on the play, and make a judgement call. Perhaps you don't want to let her go because she's good company, but is that fair to her? Is it fair to you? Maybe you're not ready to show your cards, but it comes a time when we all must decide to either fold our playing cards or show our hand.

Recognize you're wasting energy entertaining a dead-end situation. That energy could be used to create a new *game plan*–a plan to find a woman who is a better fit for you. You could also save this woman at least some of the heartache.

I recall entertaining so many dead-end situations just for the simple fact that the guy continued to amuse me. For some reason, I was intrigued that these men would say one thing, but do another. In other words, they would neither confirm nor deny they saw a future with me and their actions would lie in this gray area as well. Some days they indisputably kicked the ball in for the leading score and other days they couldn't have kicked farther from the field goal post. It was obvious there was no future in this situation, but I continued to waste my time.

If you also find yourself in a *situationship,* you're wasting your time too. If you're genuinely serious about finding a wife, think of me as your football coach. I've got a tough play for you; it's time to be MVP and execute the call. It's time to let these situations go, *Gentlemen.*

You may take an *L* in this particular game, but for your obedience, you'll earn the championship ring of marriage in the game of love. Trust and believe God has a game plan for you!

Reference

For I know the plans I have for you," says the Lord. "They are plans for good and not for disaster, to give you a future and a hope.

– Jeremiah 29:11(NKJV)

Day 18: Cuffing Season

Listen

Ne-Yo – Religious (2015)

Read

If you're a die-hard football fan, you may anxiously wait for football season. Religiously watching your team Sunday after Sunday. Just about every single man knows that with football season comes the first signs of cuffing season. The first indication of brisk fall weather starts the countdown on the scoreboard to find that special someone. If you yourself partake in cuffing season, you religiously commit yourself to the process. After years of practice, you have impeccable skills, but I'll beg to differ that your skills are as good as the *master*.

King David was the master at cuffing season, but wait, wasn't David a man after God's own heart? Yes, but His cuffing game was so strong that he had a starting lineup of many wives, concubines, and who can forget the beautiful woman by the name of Bathsheeba.

When was the last time you basked in a woman's presence and thanked God for her beauty? Be careful, there's a thin line between admiration and lust. David lusted after

Bathsheba while she was bathing (2 Samuel 11:2). In modern times, you could relate this to lusting after a woman on TV, a movie, or should I say a *flick*. You know what I mean by a flick, guys. That's right pornography.

There are many moral concerns surrounding these films, but don't worry I'm not headed there today. My intent is specifically designed for you, *Gentlemen*. Be careful who you give your praise and your hallelujah. God desires for your praise to match your actions. This means your heart should be close to Him when you praise. Your praise is not for show and should not be in vain. Jesus warned that men who were hypocrites, praying publicly just to be seen and heard, will not receive their eternal reward (Matthew 6:5). This man's reward has already been received publicly from man (Matthew 6:5).

The woman walking down the street wearing her summer sundress doesn't require your praise. Be careful what causes you to lust for it may become your idol. An idol is anything you put before God. Idolizing a woman can lead to a sin that finds you fighting an ocean's current to reach God, like Jonah. Jonah was disobedient to God and his rebellion had him dumped in the sea and swallowed up by a large fish (Jonah 1:16-17).

Sin causes distance from God. Consider David when he found himself sinning against God. He summoned

Bathsheba, which resulted in sleeping and impregnating another man's wife (2 Samuel 11:4-5). Then to cover up his sin, David plotted and successfully executed a plan to have Bathsheeba's husband killed so he may take her as his own wife (2 Samuel 11:14-27).

Of course, I'm not saying your case would be this extreme. I caution you to be careful of what you allow in your eyes' gates and ears' gates. You were born of flesh and blood. The spirit is willing, but the flesh can become weak (Matthew 26:41). Be cognizant of your surroundings and you'll lessen the blow of temptation.

God knows your heart. He knows that even when you stumble you have a heart for Him. He also will not fail to correct and convict you when you're wrong. David did not get off scot-free. God indeed punished David for conspiracy to murder Bathsheeba's husband (2 Samuel 12:10-12). You know that deep voice inside of you when you feel uneasy about your decision. That's God. Heed to that voice.

Reference

For the Lord is great and greatly to be praised;

He is to be feared above all gods.

For all the gods of the peoples are idols,

But the Lord made the heavens.

– Psalm 96:4-5 (NKJV)

Day 19: Nothing's Promised

Listen

Kanye West feat Adam Levine – Heard 'Em Say (2005)

Read

God is intentional. If you desire to live in God's image, you should also be intentional. Choose to use the day God gives you wisely. Live today because tomorrow is not promised.

My friend was preparing for his first international business assignment in the Middle East. We were discussing his upcoming trip when I asked, "Are you ready for your trip?"

He responded, "I'm treating this trip as if it's my last time in business class."

At first glance, I misinterpreted his words, thinking he was declaring this wouldn't be his last time traveling internationally in business class. I departed on a tangent about how it's great that he looks at this opportunity as just the beginning of his business class experiences. Then, I realized that's not what he anticipated at all. He expected just the opposite and he was right. He was acknowledging this opportunity as his *first time and last time*. Tomorrow is not promised. I'm confident that I'm not the only one who loses sight of the promise that another day on this earth *is not* promised (Proverbs 27:1). Be like my friend; learn to live each day to its fullest. Be humble as you welcome and appreciate each opportunity afforded to you.

Think about applying this learned concept to another dimension. Each waking morning of your life, you have another opportunity to accept Jesus Christ and live your life fulfilling His purpose. Only tomorrow morning on this earth is not promised. Understanding this fact, accept God's will for your life with today's morning breath. Your guarantee of *eternal* life depends on it.

Reference

Do not boast about tomorrow,

For you do not know what a day may bring forth.

– Proverbs 27:1 (NKJV)

Day 20: Am I A Slave?

Listen

Swoope feat. Christon Gray & Eshon Burgandy –
Dreamslave (2012)

Read

Moses' people were slaves without choice, but are you a *slave*
of choice to your belongings? Are you indebted to the new
Jordan's on a Saturday morning, or the new Call of Duty
game? Do you desire jewels that cost just as much as a brand-
new car? It's okay to desire nice things. Just make sure you
don't become a slave to *things*.

Slaves throughout history may not have had control
over their own lives, but if they had nothing else they had
their faith and their faith did not fail them. In the story of
Moses, the Hebrew slaves were set free (Exodus 13:3) and
their future generations possessed the legacy of freedom in
the promised land (Joshua 1:4).

Even men who were free throughout history
understood the blessed consequences of choosing to follow
God. Abraham's legacy was the father of many nations
because he chose to serve and trust God (Genesis 17:4). Jesus
became our Savior, who ascended from this world, leaving us

with a concrete example of how to live our lives daily (Acts 1:9). For this reason, we are baptized and all one in Christ (Galatians 3:26-28).

You may also desire to leave a legacy; a sense of inheritance, and entitlement to your children and children's children. We all know what we earn can't come with us to the grave. Remember the greatest legacy you can offer to your family is the inheritance to know and serve God. Investing in your legacy starts today not when you have your first child or marry your wife. Choose today to grant your legacy permission to take roots and it will blossom and bloom throughout every generation that follows you. This is true freedom! This is the true salvation.

Reference

For to me, to live *is* Christ, and to die *is* gain.

– Philippians 1:21 (NKJV)

Day 21: Run, Forrest, Run!

Listen

T-Pain feat. Wiz Khalifa & Lily Allen – 5 O' Clock (2011)

Read

As we enter into this next devotion, I pray that you are not led into temptation, but delivered from evil (Matthew 6:13). I introduce this devotion with scripture because this is no easy message to deliver to you. *Gentlemen,* this is something that both men and women have struggled with since the beginning of time.

In my opinion, it's one of the greatest temptations known to man, even more tempting than when Eve ate the fruit of the tree of knowledge of good and evil. Yes, this temptation is all around us. You hear about it in songs on the radio, you see it on the television, and you may even converse about it with your friends after a game of basketball.

You may have guessed it. It's three little words that carry such a heavy weight. Those 3 letters spell s-e-x.

Although the Holy Bible implies no sin is greater than the other (Romans 3:23, Romans 6:23), sex is a sin categorized like no other. This sin is a transgression against your own body (1 Corinthians 6:18). Yes, for men too. One common misconception is that sex doesn't affect men the way it does women, but this is not according to God's Word.

Just through committing yourself to this journey, you have taken a conscious step toward living a life amidst God. Your old life has been washed away and you have become a new man–a *Gentleman* of God (2 Corinthians 5:17).

Since you are choosing to seek God in all aspects of your life, including matters of the heart, you'll find with no doubt that you'll also have to face the question of God's desire for celibacy in your life. You'll need to make up in your own mind that celibacy is the way you will live your life. Not just that, you'll need to determine if celibacy is really the way you *want* to live your life–especially when you receive a tempting invitation to meet a woman in her bedroom at 5 o'clock in the morning.

These are no easy decisions, but even if you make the attempt to ask God into your life, but still try to keep God out of your sex life, you will find that your thoughts on the subject will have no choice but to become elevated.

If you need some help living out a decision of celibacy, seek God. If you have fallen for this temptation, ask God for forgiveness for sinning against your own body. When you find yourself facing this temptation, run! Run as fast as you do down a basketball court to shoot a basket or run as fast as you can run a lap around the track. If you need to, run like Forrest Gump! Run, Forrest run!

Pray for a heart's desire to serve God and to conduct yourself in His holiness. Flee from temptation. God is faithful. If you pay close attention, you'll see that God will give you a way out (1 Corinthians 10:13). It may come in the form of a phone call right before you decide to make that tempting choice. It may come in just a second thought that crosses your mind. Recognize this as your way out. You still have a chance to change the fate of your decision.

Consider your end goal; you desire a God-ordained marriage. Although tomorrow is not promised, there's no telling what today's pleasure can bring you tomorrow. Sexual sin is known to bring forth children out of wedlock, diseases, and personal stress. These consequences are not sins in and of themselves, but these outcomes stem from sin that can potentially delay your blessing of a wife.

If you're like me, I want my blessing and I want it now. If being obedient to God's way means I can receive my blessing with greater haste, then I'll do everything in my power to do things according to God's will the first time. *Gentlemen*, ask yourself if you're willing to do the same.

Reference

Run from sexual sin! No other sin so clearly affects the body as this one does. For sexual immorality is a sin against your own body. Don't you realize that your body is the temple of the Holy Spirit, who lives in you and was given to you by God? You do not belong to yourself, for God bought you with a high price. So you must honor God with your body.

– 1 Corinthians 6:18-20 (NLT)

Day 22: Netflix and Chill?

Listen

Beyoncé feat. Jay Z – Drunk in Love [Clean] (2013)

Read

Let's face it, temptation is everywhere. There's no avoiding it altogether so how do you know where to draw the line?

When I hosted *Single Ladies* events for *The Single Ladies' Commandments*, I always welcomed interaction. It's not always enough for me to sit up in front of a crowd and talk at people. I want dialogue. I want to communicate. I like to listen, provide feedback, and vice versa. Then, we will start the process all over again. This is a classic case of communication.

When someone shows up at one of my hosted events, I realize they're not always willing to raise their hand to speak up. To counteract that, I sometimes offer anonymous means to share questions or comments.

At my first book release party, I recall one of my guest's questions in particular. On the small pink notecard, this *Single Ladies'* question read: "When dating, when is a good time to invite someone to your home?" I'll admit I was a little taken aback. I had no idea that releasing this book would lead

70

to relationship questions. I've been single for years. I mean almost a decade. I know how to be single; I can encourage anyone through singleness. If you ask me to give you advice on how to lay the foundation of a successful relationship in the future, I thought, *well I have an opinion, not sure if it's the right answer.* I had to come to terms with the fact that God was calling me to share my expertise.

After careful thought and a quick prayer, I answered this question. Perhaps my question is a cop out because my honest answer is there is no conclusive answer. The answer really lies with the two-people undertaking the dating experience.

If we really want to dive deep into this question, we need to first understand the foundation. You have to understand if you are dating this woman, or courting this woman, you both have to be on the same page. One person can't be dating, while the other is courting.

Courting is just another form of dating. It's dating with a purpose and intent that you two have the same end goal in mind. The agreed upon objective must be communicated with one another and not assumed. The end goal of courting is often most associated with marriage, while dating can be a more casual experience. You may have begun dating at 16 years old. You were just trying to understand what you like or dislike in a partner. You sought this dating experience in order to get to know a young lady on a different level outside of a *platonic* friendship. This didn't necessarily mean that at 16 years of age you both had intentions to marry each other one day.

Circling back to our *Single Ladies'* question, when should you ask a woman to come over for an evening of *Netflix and Chill?* Hopefully, you never do. I don't mean you never ask her to visit you at your home. However, you know as well as I do, the chill part usually doesn't mean just *chilling.* With that being said, if chilling is indeed dating that person for a few weeks or months, and then results in you enjoying each other's company in the privacy of your own home or hers, then I see nothing wrong with this intention.

However, you both need to have a conversation to ensure you're on the same page. Do you share the same morals? Do you both desire celibacy? Will you respect each other's boundaries and avoid a temptation that will cause you to sin against God? These are the questions you must ask yourself and of each other. The last thing you want is to wake up *drunk in love* the next morning on the kitchen floor because you didn't have this conversation.

If you know partaking in alcoholic beverages during your evening date indoors will have you tempted to cross the line, make sure you have a conversation with the woman upfront. Perhaps you limit your intake or remove the risk of indulging all together. Commit yourself to being drunk in the Spirit instead of *drunk in love*.

Above all, make sure your thoughts line up with God and you can prove so through your actions. Ultimately, you'll know for yourself when it's the right time to invite a woman to your home without sacrificing your salvation.

Reference

And do not be drunk with wine, in which is dissipation; but be filled with the Spirit.

– Ephesians 5:18 (NKJV)

.

Commandment #4

Purpose

Thou shall trust God for divine *purpose.*

Day 23: Dreaming Out Loud

Listen

Owl City – Fireflies (2009)

Read

If you're familiar with the guidance of some male relationship experts, they inform women that men are not willing to settle down unless they first have their own life completely in order. I'll just say this is not my experience.

More than a few men have asked for my hand in dating even when they didn't have much going for them. I know women who have experienced similar situations; including guys who had nothing going for them, calling collect from a prison phone, or fresh out of prison.

This is not the norm, but my point is I'm familiar with cases where guys are still seeking love even if they're not in the best of circumstances. Some men are *broke* college students, have a low-income job, or no job at all, yet and still manage to muster up the financial means and courage to ask women out. Consequently, I say to the relationship experts who claim a man won't seriously date a woman unless his life is in order, I call your bluff. In fact, I call it *fluff*. In other words, I just don't buy it!

With that being said, you, *Gentlemen* have inspirations and dreams. Some dreams you may lack the funds or the motivation to support it. Occasionally, you still date women without your necessities in order because you're natural seekers who still desire love, even when you may be lacking a life's purpose. Maybe you think if you had a woman beside you, supporting you, you would gain that motivation. You would be inspired to seek creative ways to fund your dream.

I'm here to tell you that if God placed a vision inside of you, He is just and right to fulfill it. You may feel as if you don't have the qualifications–the best education, the best credit for a loan, or the right support system. It's easy to look at what you don't have, but recognize what you do possess. You have God! There is a reason your dreams are bursting at the seams. That reason is that *God doesn't always call the qualified, but He qualifies those who He has called* (Romans 8:30). *God promises that all things work together for good to them that love God, to them who are the called according to His purpose* (Romans 8:28 NKJV).

Take Moses for instance, he wasn't born an eloquent orator. In fact, he had a speech impediment (Exodus 4:10). Moses stuttered. Can you imagine Pharaoh sitting there waiting for Moses as he stammered to declare God's decree to *let My people go*? Do you recall the Holy Bible even mentioning his handicap during these bouts with Pharaoh? This answer is, no. Do you know why? God equipped Moses with the ability to push through this challenge and achieve his divine purpose despite his personal opposition. Indeed, *Gentlemen,* you can do the same!

All you need is a vision and a plan. Do as Daniel; he had a dream, and then he proceeded to write it down (Daniel 7:1). Follow your plan with diligence. Seek God for direction and lean on God for His understanding as you execute.

Reference

Then the Lord answered me and said:

"Write the vision

And make it plain on tablets,

That he may run who reads it."

– Habakkuk 2:2 (NKJV)

Day 24: You Go Boy!

Listen

Aloe Blacc – The Man (2013)

Read

Some women may try to take a man's place as fathers and even as men, but *Gentlemen,* women can never replace you no matter how hard we try. That means we need you. We need you to be the man God called you on this earth to be. We need you to be strong, confident, and bold walking in God's wisdom and obedient to His calling on your life.

You must be swift, a great force, an unhinged fire, and mysterious, yet debonair. Do you understand why this is so important? Your enemy tries to mirror all these characteristics. This means you have to be a greater component–more cunning and more spiritually raging.

Temptresses and men may attempt to distract you and plot against you. You may be surprised to find when these men are people you call your friends, bosses, or brothers, but these men are not your real enemy. We do not battle against flesh and blood, but rulers, principalities (Ephesians 6:12). This means your enemy is Satan and his angels who fell from Heaven and God's good grace (Ezekiel

28:14-18).

God needs you to be strong enough to stand against the enemy. Not only does God need you, but we as women need you. We live in a world where *Single Ladies* are quick to throw that left hand in the air to show off their unmarried status. Women may be quick to say they do not need a man nor do they want a man. We don't live in a world like your father or father's father where women wanted to stay home, raise the children, and be caretakers of the household.

Speaking first-hand, *Single Ladies* are independent, but we still have the desire for you to be our husbands, fathers to our children, and providers both financially and spiritually. In the early stages of the Garden of Eden, Adam desired companionship. I'm sure once Eve was created, she desired this same sense of companionship as well.

Today, we are just descendants of Adam and Eve that desire the same thing. Only today, it's not so easy. Women just don't find themselves in your garden when you wake in the morning ready to take on the world alongside you. It's much more challenging, but we will not and can't afford to accept a man who has not proven himself to be a man of God. This is a man who loves God, a man who daily seeks His purpose, and follows God in all His plans.

You may feel you did not have positive male role

models to guide you to becoming this type of man.

Understand God gave you plenty of examples of men with these qualities in the Holy Bible; Noah, Job, and John the Baptist just to name a few. The most notable example of this man will always be Jesus Christ–a man who came down to earth, so you may have life more abundantly (John 10:10).

The question is, are you ready to accept this abundant life? You already have the tools in front of you. It's just a matter of making the decision to become the man God called you to be and walking into your pre-destined role, *Gentlemen*.

I'll give you a few tips to help you take advantage of this destiny. A God-fearing man should aspire to be definite, consistent, and leaning on the promises of God. You do not have to swear by anything. Jesus told us the importance of being confident in our yes or no (Matthew 5:37).

As *Gentlemen*, you should learn that every *no* doesn't require an explanation. If you're uncomfortable or you know you can't commit, exercise your right to say no. Non-clarity leads to confusion. Recognize the enemy is the source of confusion and not of God (1 Corinthians 14:33). Therefore, be concise and be truthful.

Recognize you're the clay (Isaiah 64:8). God is the potter. You're the man who God broke the mold when He created you. That means you're unique. You're a blessed man of God. You're *The Man.* You go boy!

Reference

You made all the delicate, inner parts of my body

and knit me together in my mother's womb.

Thank you for making me so wonderfully complex!

Your workmanship is marvelous—how well I know it.

You watched me as I was being formed in utter seclusion,

as I was woven together in the dark of the womb.

You saw me before I was born.

Every day of my life was recorded in your book.

Every moment was laid out

before a single day had passed.

— Psalm 139:13-16 (NLT)

Day 25: Superman

Listen

Tye Tribbett & G.A. – Look Up (2008)

Read

Look up! *It's a bird. It's a plane. It's Superman.*

When all else fails, look up. Look up to the One who is there to help you. Look up to the hills. This is where your help comes from.

Life is hard work, but when you have God on your side the burdens of life become lighter. Look up to the One who created the heavens, earth, and everything in it within seven days' time.

What can you do in a week? The number seven is symbolical of perfect completion and creation both in the spiritual and physical world. Some may say, *'well, God really created the world in six days, not seven days.'* You may have a point there, but there's a reason seven days is emphasized. God showed us how important it is to rest.

Gentlemen, you can be out here pushing, pulling, and advocating for your dreams. You may even flaunt *a-no-days-off* approach, but remember even God rested. As the book of Genesis reads, "On the seventh day God ended His work

83

which He had done, and He rested on the seventh day from all His work which He had done," (Genesis 2:2 NKJV).

Use your full week to the best of your ability. Use your days strategically with a purpose. Do your due diligence, plan for the days you will work, and plan for the days you will rest.

This is important for both your physical and mental health. It becomes more challenging for God to invite you to your calling if you're always burned out and overwhelmed. *Gentlemen,* I know there are times you feel like Superman up in the sky soaring and saving the world, but even Clark Kent knew he needed work-life balance. He knew there was a time to save the world, a time to work at the *Daily Star* newspaper, and a time to spend with Lois. Balance is a major key, *Gentlemen.*

Reference

I will lift up my eyes to the hills—
From whence comes my help?
My help comes from the Lord,
Who made heaven and earth.
– Psalm 121:1-2 (NKJV)

Day 26: Trap Queen

Listen

Mali Music – Royalty (2014)

Read

Gentlemen, let me introduce you to a well-known *Trap Queen*. This queen came along long before today's idea of a *Trap Queen*. In fact, this queen lived thousands of years ago.

Esther was the second woman in the Holy Bible to have her name grace a book. God positioned Esther as queen of many lands making her the ultimate *Trap Queen*. In other words, this woman was loyal and resourceful. In this sense, much like the most *powerful women* you can think of today.

I'm just going to tell you now, *Gentlemen*, you need to get yourself an Esther. Esther was a woman who made a conscious choice to live in her divine purpose. God strategically positioned Esther in a worldly role of authority as she was a favored woman of God.

When it came time to speak up for her people, God's people, she was obedient to God. She spoke to the king on behalf of the Jews, and the king honored her request (Esther 5:1-8).

She knew if she did not speak up, God would call another woman to perform His decree to save His people (Esther 4:13-14). This example shows us that we are designed for God's purpose and we should seek ways to fulfill that purpose. God has also called you, *Gentlemen,* for such a time as this (Esther 4:14 NKJV).

In this world, God-fearing *Gentlemen* are often looked at as the silent minority. Don't believe me? Attend a church with a large congregation on any given Sunday and look around. What will you see? In many cases, you'll see more women than men. Churches are always seeking creative and insightful ways to draw you inside and sometimes to no avail.

This is because God needs His men—His kings. He needs you to lead and not just in the church, but in your current position in life. Like Esther, you are also chosen royalty. You are appointed and anointed to minister. You are a minister of God exactly where you are. In your daily profession and in every encounter in life, He needs you to be the change agent in your environment.

This book is a testament of how God can use any mechanism or tool he sees fit to foster His vision into fruition. This book stands in the gap of two worlds: contemporary music and biblical scripture. When I first began marketing this book series, it was clear to me that I was walking on unchartered territory. In some instances, the world didn't want to touch my book for fear I would slip up and push God's agenda. Due to this, I *lost* opportunities with public media platforms. When I requested air time with Christian-based avenues, some declined as they were quite perplexed that the book included *secular* music.

With so much rejection, I could have given up on continuing to write this book series, but I trust God. I take comfort in that the readers and platforms, who have and will take an interest in my books, will find it a blessing. I understand living in my purpose increases my life's satisfaction. I'm happier living in my purpose. I also understand there are consequences for not acting on the vision God instilled in me.

Have you ever had an idea or an invention that you thought of, and then some time later you see someone else do it? Understand if you don't act on your vision, God will call other *Gentlemen* to fulfill His purpose. You may face challenges and adversity on your road to living your purpose out loud, but trust God and believe He has the final say. He will open doors and grant you favor in ways you could have never imagined. All you have to do is trust God for the vision and walk according to His calling. Use your power justly to make an impact on this world. Oh, and find yourself a *Trap*

Queen like Esther who will support your dream.

Reference

"For if you remain completely silent at this time, relief and deliverance will arise for the Jews from another place, but you and your father's house will perish. Yet who knows whether you have come to the kingdom for such a time as this?"

– Esther 4:14 (NKJV)

Day 27: Finally Famous

Listen

Andy Mineo – Dunk Contest (Magic Bird) (2017)

Read

Looking at my handwriting today, you may never have guessed that I failed fifth-grade cursive handwriting assignments. That summer following the fifth grade, I vowed that my handwriting would never fail me again.

That's not to say seven years of taking rapid notes in college didn't change my handwriting drastically and that in a rush my *pen-womanship* is scribbly chicken scratch only I can interpret. It is to say that I worked hard to perfect my cursive writing. No matter how obsolete cursive is considered today, there's just something special to me about writing an elegant note.

When I slow down, take my time, and place a pen in my hand, my writing has been described as art or calligraphy. A beautiful expression of how words can flow so eloquently off a ballpoint pen.

As I mentioned, it was not always this way. Math assignments always came easy to me. A good grasp of science ensued once I passed grade school. I was a great reader, maybe a little shaky in my language arts comprehension, but still ahead of my class. Handwriting? That was mediocre.

That summer after fifth grade, I practiced. That's right, I practiced my handwriting day in and day out until I got it just where I wanted it. I entered the sixth grade with handwriting so beautiful the girls were jealous, and the guys swooned. Perhaps I'm being a little dramatic. Okay, I'm being dramatic. I'm pretty sure no girl has ever been green with envy over my script and no guy fell head over heels in love with me because of my transcribing either.

I write all this to say that practice makes perfect. If you have a desire, but lack the skillset, seek opportunities to gain proficiency. If you have to sign up for a college course, do it. If you need to engage the time of a mentor, make it happen. Do you need special tutoring or coaching? Invest in yourself. Whatever you need to do to get to where you're going is likely going to take hard work.

LeBron James and Steph Curry may make it look like the basketball just magically flows out of their hand and floats perfectly into the basket, but we are talking about practice here. Yes, Allen Iverson said it best, *"We're talking about practice."* Mr. Iverson was disputing the need for practice in his *now infamous* interview. For our purposes, we are going to agree practice is everything!

Magic and Shaq couldn't win dunk contests or become legends in their own right without practice. Likewise, if you want to be *finally famous* in your own right, you better get in the zone and practice! Practice like your life depends on it. If you get weary, you can recover quickly. If you take a hard loss, focus on bouncing back from your circumstances. Seek God for strength. Keep moving and keep practicing.

Reference

Work hard so you can present yourself to God and receive his approval. Be a good worker, one who does not need to be ashamed and who correctly explains the word of truth.

– 2 Timothy 2:15 (NKJV)

Day 28: Count Your Blessings

Listen

Lecrae (feat. Ty Dolla $ign) – Blessings (2017)

Read

Rejection is an integral part of the process of life, but a hard and painful pill to swallow. Rejection may come in the form of you asking a woman out on a date, but she gracefully declines. It may come in the form of an email regretting that you were not amongst the most qualified candidates for your dream job.

Rejection will always be there to rear its ugly head, but who said it has to be so ugly. Rejection can also be a form of protection. What if that woman who declined your date was worse than Delilah? What if that job would have led to a layoff only 3 months down the road?

You just never know what God is protecting you from, both seen and unseen. That *loss* may just be a blessing in disguise. I ask you, *Gentlemen,* to trust God. It's true, rejection can be disheartening, but you know what's more disheartening? Living a life that is not lining up in God's will or not walking in your true God-given calling because you forged a path that God never intended you to travel.

This doesn't mean God won't call you to travel the road less traveled. Sometimes God requires us to put in the work because *faith without works is dead* (James 2:14-18 NKJV).

Jesus explained, "For assuredly, I say to you, if you have faith as a mustard seed, you will say to this mountain, 'Move from here to there,' and it will move; and nothing will be impossible for you," (Matthew 17:20). You too can have the faith the size of a muster seed, but if you don't put in the effort to make things happen, all that faith is useless. Work your faith. Count the many blessings you already have all around you. Put that faith into action and watch how God shows up and shows out in your life!

Reference

Therefore, having been justified by faith, we have peace with God through our Lord Jesus Christ through whom also we have access by faith into this grace in which we stand, and rejoice in hope of the glory of God. And not only *that*, but we also glory in tribulations, knowing that tribulation produces perseverance; and perseverance, character; and character, hope. Now hope does not disappoint because the love of God has been poured out in our hearts by the Holy Spirit who was given to us.

– Romans 5:1-5 (NKJV)

Day 29: Falsehood

Listen

J. Cole – False Prophets [Clean] (2016)

Read

In whatever you do and whoever you are, understand it's the God in you that has gotten you this far. In other words, whoever you are, be a good one!

Be careful of who you keep in your circle. Everyone does not have your best intentions at heart. Some people are wolves disguised as sheep. *Beware of false prophets who come disguised as harmless sheep but are really vicious wolves* (Matthew 7:15 NLT).

Gentlemen, be mindful of the company you keep. The enemy sends deceitful women, dishonest men, and even fraudulent prophets falsely promising you peace and blessings (Jeremiah 8:10-12; Jeremiah 23:16-18).

Jesus warned, *for false christs and false prophets will rise and show great signs and wonders to deceive, if possible, even the elect* (Matthew 24:24 NKJV).

Many will come claiming the end of times in Jesus' name (Matthew 24:5-6). Don't be worried or anxious, only God knows the time when this earth shall pass away (Mark

13:32-33).

As you learned, your eyes' gates are a direct connection to your spirit. When your eyes are exposed to things that are corrupt, you may also become corrupt or disturbed on the inside (Luke 11:34). If your eyes receive things that are righteous, you will exuberate righteousness (Luke 11:34).

In the same token, the things that you hear may affect you. Be careful of what you listen to and what gets into your spirit. Be watchful of what you allow in your life, as distractions can sidetrack you from your purpose.

Reference

Depart from evil and do good;

Seek peace [in God] and pursue it.

– Psalm 34:14 (NKJV)

Day 30: SME

Listen

Trip Lee – Sweet Victory (2014)

Read

Become an expert. A common misconception is that an expert has to know everything!

A Subject Matter Expert (SME) is someone who has knowledge of a particular subject very well. A SME is also someone who knows where to seek information that they do not know. A SME is strategic and resourceful.

Well, what if you have full knowledge of your passion, but haven't taken the leap from novice to expertise. Understand *there is nothing new under the sun* (Ecclesiastes 1:9 NKJV).

Collaborate with experts in your field; follow them on social media, read their books, and benchmark them. Seek ways to set yourself apart, build your own brand, and develop a plan to breakthrough. This means you seek methods to surpass, not match, those who share a passion for this similar expertise.

Most importantly, seek God. Inquire with the Lord before you enter into a new endeavor. Pray. In a time of war,

David's wives were captured and held captive. Before charging in to retrieve them, David inquired with the Lord.

"Shall I pursue this troop? Shall I overtake them?" he asked the Lord.

"Pursue, for you shall surely overtake them and without fail recover *all*," He answered back (1 Samuel 30:8 NKJV).

In my Bible, the word *all* is italicized, meaning there is emphasis on all! If we seek Him first, God will keep no good thing from us (Psalm 84:11).

Don't be afraid to approach God's throne in humility and ask. Sometimes the reason you lack is because you do not seek God and simply make your request. Other times, you may ask, but you're waiting on God's perfect timing.

You can also apply this request to seeking a wife. If you have a woman that you desire to pursue as a wife, ask God if this is a woman you should pursue. Seek His counsel in all things and you can't fail, *Gentlemen*.

Do you know your words are so powerful? If you want it, say it! Sometimes we are afraid to open up our mouths and speak. We may pray to God inwardly, but we fear to speak up outwardly. God has equipped you with the words to speak, but you're withholding them. You're not using one of your most powerful tools as *Gentlemen*. You're withholding your spoken word! When you reserve your words, you may be prolonging your own God-ordained blessings.

Are you speaking victory over your heart's desires? As *Gentlemen,* you should speak bravely over your desires by humbly reaching God in prayer. Speak to God and request those things in faith as if they have already come into fruition (Romans 4:17). Speak life and positivity over all things concerning you! Don't forget you must also put action behind those words.

Be the SME of your own life! After all, it's a subject you know very well. You have the exact expertise to express what you need and desire.

With God, you will win the fight for bragging rights and sweet victory. God didn't promise the road will be easy, but He has already equipped you with the full armor of God. All you need to do is pick up your armor, go forth, spread your wings, and be prepared to battle for your promises of **love**, **healing**, **freedom**, and **purpose**, *Gentlemen!*

Reference

Therefore put on the full armor of God, so that when the day of evil comes, you may be able to stand your ground, and after you have done everything, to stand. Stand therefore, having girded your waist with truth, having put on the breastplate of righteousness, and having shod your feet with the preparation of the gospel of peace; above all, taking the shield of faith with which you will be able to quench all the fiery darts of the wicked one. And take the helmet of salvation, and the sword of the Spirit, which is the word of God; praying always with all prayer and supplication in the Spirit, being watchful to this end with all perseverance and supplication for all the saints— and for me, that utterance may be given to me, that I may open my mouth boldly to make known the mystery of the gospel, for which I am an ambassador in chains; that in it I may speak boldly, as I ought to speak.

– Ephesians 6:13-20 (NKJV)

You can find out more about

Jasmine Jones

and her books at www.jasminejones.co

Follow Jasmine Jones!

www.facebook.com/jasminejones.co

www.instagram.com/jasminejones.co

www.twitter.com/jasminejonesco

For information, questions, scheduling, or details about
upcoming books in The Commandments Series, please
contact the author at the email provided
info@jasminejones.co, or visit www.jasminejones.co.

About the Author

Author of *The Commandments Series*, Jasmine Jones, engages an interest and love for contemporary music and biblical scripture in *The Single Ladies' Commandments: Songs for Love, Healing, Freedom, and Purpose* and *The Gentlemen's Commandments: Songs for Love, Healing, Freedom, and Purpose*. In her short story, *"911" Emergency Crisis: The Day I Lost My Mind, Literally*, Jasmine vividly shares her transparent testimony of becoming an author and chief executive visionary of J Squared Productions, a business solutions company that cultivates an engineering approach to book publishing, marketing, and product development.

An engineer at a Fortune 500 automotive company in Detroit, Michigan, Jasmine earned dual Bachelor of Science degrees in Industrial Operations Engineering and Mechanical Engineering with summa cum laude and honors from Lawrence Technological University and a Master's in Engineering Management from the Pennsylvania State University.

Jasmine balances her many roles with time dedicated to traveling, writing, and STEMulating and mentoring young people in science, technology, engineering, and mathematics. As a result of her service to the community, Jasmine, a member of Alpha Kappa Alpha Sorority, Inc. and National of Society of Black Engineers, was the recipient of several organization awards. Formerly competing in Miss America Scholarship pageants, Jasmine was the recipient of the Miss Michigan Scholarship Pageant National Academic Scholarship Award and held the title of Miss Lawrence Tech in 2011.